AF270805

FRANKENSTEIN

by
Mary Shelley

Student Packet

Written by
Gloria Levine, M. A.

Contains masters for:	2	Prereading Activities
	1	Study Guide
	4	Vocabulary Activities
	2	Literary Analysis Activities
	4	Critical Thinking Activities
	3	Writing Activities
	1	Review Crossword
	2	Comprehension Quizzes (Levels I and II)
	2	Novel Tests (Levels I and II)
PLUS		Detailed Answer Key

Note

The text used to prepare this guide was the Bantam Classic softcover. It was first published in 1818. If other editions are used, page references may vary slightly.

Please note: Please assess the appropriateness of this book for the age level and maturity of your students prior to reading and discussing it with your class.

ISBN 978-1-56137-751-0

To order, contact your local school supply store, or—

Novel Units, Inc.
P.O. Box 97
Bulverde, TX 78163-0097

Web site: novelunits.com

Monday

Name _____

8/20/14

Anticipation Guide

Directions: Rate each of the following statements before you read the novel, and discuss your ratings with a partner. After you have completed the novel, rate and discuss the statements again.

1 ———— 2 ———— 3 ———— 4 ———— 5 ———— 6
strongly agree   strongly disagree

	Before	After
1. Technology will eventually solve most of our problems.	6	
2. Medical researchers will eventually find cures for the major ailments.	6	
3. Aging and death are a part of the natural cycle; we will never find a way to avoid them.	1	
4. Scientists should be given more freedom.	3.5	
5. Scientists should not be held responsible for the ways their discoveries are put to use.	3	
6. Parents should be held accountable for their children's misbehavior.	2	
7. Being a parent is a big responsibility.	1	
8. People with physical deformities are often mistreated because others fear them.	4	
9. Everyone has the right to become a parent.	3.5	
10. Companionship is a basic need that is as important as food or shelter.	5	
11. I like a scary story.	3.5	
12. Frankenstein's monster was evil.	6	
13. Everyone has a good side and a bad side.	2	
14. If you're accused but innocent, justice will prevail.	3.5	
15. People tend to get nasty in a crowd.	3	
16. Pursuit of knowledge should be for the purpose of improving the world.	6	

Name _____

8/20/14

Directions: Several journal entries have been started for you below. Add a few of your thoughts to each one.

1. Frankenstein…

    was the scientist who created life from dead things in the story.

    _____

2. In my worst nightmare…

    I don't have a "worst" nothing.

3. It was a nightmare-come-true the day I…

    is not to mean widely used when talking about petty things.

    _____

4. A monster…

    is when being deemed out of the ordinary, or threatening, inhuman.

    _____

5. The most horrible thing that ever happened to me…

    Again, no "worst or best".

    _____

6. I am afraid…

    of heights, spiders, and things that do not concern you

7. The difference between fear and disgust…

    is that people now rather be disgusted than afraid.

    _____

8. If a way were found to prevent all sickness…

    ~~xxxxxxxxxxxx~~ we would be in a frightful.

    _____

© Novel Units, Inc.

Name _____

Directions: On separate paper, write a brief answer to each study question as you read the novel at home or in class. Use the questions for review before group discussions and before your final test. Starred questions have no "right" or "wrong" answers.

* = thought or opinion question

** = prediction

Letters 1–4

1. Who is R. Walton and why is he writing to his sister?

2. What did R. Walton love to read about when he was a boy?

3. What career did R. Walton pursue unsuccessfully for a year before inheriting his cousin's fortune?

4. What does R. Walton tell his sister is the "one want which I have never yet been able to satisfy"? (p. 4)

5. Why did R. Walton decide to hire the man who is now master of the ship?

6. What strange sight did R. Walton and his men see with their telescopes as they waited for the fog to clear?

7. What was odd about the stranger's asking where the ship was going before he consented to come on board?

8. What did the stranger answer when asked why he had come so far on the ice?

* 9. What is it about the stranger that Captain Walton finds so interesting and appealing? What is it about the Captain that makes the stranger so gloomy and upset?

** 10. Prediction: What will the stranger's story be about?

Chapters 1–4

1. Whose relationship is the stranger describing when he says, "He strove to shelter her, as a fair exotic is sheltered by the gardener..." (p. 19)?

2. How did the stranger's parents treat him when he was a child?

3. Why did the peasant family raise Elizabeth—and why did they give her up?

4. To what native country did Victor's parents return to raise their children?

5. Who was Victor's close boyhood friend?

6. When he was 15, what did Victor see that made him doubt that the ancient philosophers who had so intrigued him could ever provide real knowledge?

7. How did Victor's mother die?

8. Who told Victor he was "happy to have gained a disciple" (p. 34)?

* 9. "Although I possessed the capacity of bestowing animation, yet to prepare a frame for the reception of it....still remained a work of inconceivable difficulty and labour" (p. 38). What was Victor saying—and in what tone of voice do you imagine him saying it?

** 10. Prediction: Will Victor's father learn what his son is up to at school?

Chapters 5–7 Wednesday

1. How did Victor spend the night after bringing the creature to life?

2. How much did Victor confide to his friend Clerval about bringing the creature to life?

3. What is Victor describing when he says that "surely nothing but the unbounded and unremitting attentions of my friend could have restored me to life" (p. 47)?

4. What did Elizabeth say about Justine in her letter to Victor?

5. After his recuperation, what did Victor decide to study alongside of Clerval?

6. Why was Victor in such a good mood right before getting the upsetting letter from his father?

7. According to the letter from Victor's father, what happened to William?

8. Where did Victor see the creature again, several months after creating him?

* 9. What would Victor's family have said if he had told them why he was so sure that Justine was innocent?

** 10. Prediction: Will Justine be executed or set free?

Chapters 8–11 Thur

1. Why did it look as if Justine were the murderer?

2. What did Elizabeth say to the court in Justine's defense?

3. Why did Justine confess and what was the result?

4. "When I reflected on his crimes...I would have made a pilgrimage to the highest peak of the Andes, could I when there have precipitated him to their base." (p. 76) How did Victor feel about his creation—and why didn't he hunt down the creature?

5. Where did Victor next see the creature and why didn't he take the opportunity to destroy his creation?

6. What deal did the creature make with Victor?

7. What did the creature tell Victor about how he spent the first weeks after his creation?

8. Briefly describe the cottagers living next to the creature's refuge.

* 9. Write down one or two sentences that show the creature's positive feelings toward the cottagers as he observes them.

** 10. Prediction: How will the cottagers react when they lay eyes on the creature?

Name _____

Chapters 12–15 *Friday A*

1. Why did the creature stop taking food from the cottagers' store?

2. How did the creature learn to speak?

3. How did the creature learn to read?

4. How did the creature learn what he looked like?

5. List two favors the creature did for the cottagers.

6. Why did Felix cheer up in the spring?

7. How did the De Lacey family lose their money?

8. What was the creature's reaction to *Paradise Lost*?

 * 9. Reread pp. 117–120, in which the creature shows himself to the cottagers. Copy a part of that description that sticks in your mind for some reason—and tell why.

** 10. Prediction: Where will the creature go now?

Chapters 16–19 *Mon*

1. How did the creature learn that the cottagers had moved out of their cottage?

2. Where did the creature decide to go after burning the cottage?

3. The creature says that "a circumstance that happened when I arrived on the confines of Switzerland...confirmed...the bitterness and horror of my feelings" (p. 125). What happened?

4. How did the creature get revenge when he arrived in Geneva?

5. Why did the creature want Justine to suffer and how did he decide to accomplish that?

6. What reason did Victor give the creature for refusing to create a female?

7. "After ...reflection, I concluded that the justice due both to him and my fellow creatures demanded of me that I should comply with his request" (p. 133). Briefly explain.

8. Why did Victor return to England?

 * 9. Cite a line that conveys how much Victor dreaded the work he was doing on the female.

** 10. Prediction: What will happen when the creature comes to claim the female that Victor Frankenstein is making?

Chapters 20–22 *Tue*

1. List two fears Victor had about creating a female creature.

2. What did Victor do when he saw the creature watching him work on the female?

3. How did Victor interpret the creature's threat, "...remember, I shall be with you on your wedding night"?

4. When Victor entered the harbor to ask directions, why did the stranger answer rudely, "Maybe you are come to a place that will not prove much to your taste..." (p. 157)?

5. How did Clerval die?

6. How was Victor's reaction to Clerval's death like his reaction when the creature was brought to life?

7. Who was Mr. Kirwin and how did he treat Victor?

8. What was the contrast in mood between Victor's father and his bride on the day that Victor and Elizabeth were married?

* 9. What do you think would have happened if Victor had given the female to the creature and let them go on their way?

** 10. Prediction: What will happen the day after Victor's wedding?

Chapters 23–24

1. When Victor heard his bride scream, "the whole truth rushed into [his] mind" (p. 179). Briefly explain what he realized.

2. How did Victor's father react to the news that Elizabeth was dead?

3. Why did Victor describe the creature to the magistrate?

4. Why did Victor travel for several months after Elizabeth's murder?

5. Why did the creature sometimes leave Victor messages about where to find food?

6. What does Victor ask Walton to promise, if Victor dies while the monster still lives?

7. What are Victor's and Walton's reactions when the men make their demand to return home?

8. How did the creature react when he found Victor dead?

* 9. Why didn't Walton kill the creature?

** 10. Prediction: What do you suppose happens to the creature after he is borne away by the waves?

Name _____

Analogies

forebodings	sledges	mariner	gales
apparition	draught	fastidious	lineaments
interment	penury	rustic	sepulchre
metaphysical	inclemency	slough	galvanism
progeny	omen	malignity	prognosticated
alchemists	benevolence	panegyric	transmuted

Directions: An analogy is a comparison. For example:

NO is to **YES** as **OFF** is to **ON**.
HILL is to **MOUNTAIN** as **STREAM** is to **RIVER**.

Use words from the vocabulary box to complete the anlogies, below. Then create two of your own for a classmate to solve.

1. PRESERVED is to SAME as _____ is to DIFFERENT.

2. LABOR is to TOIL as _____ is to TOMB.

3. CRITICISM is to CENSURE as COMMENDATION is to _____.

4. DRUGS are to PHARMACOTHERAPY as ELECTRICITY is to

   _____.

5. OPULENCE is to WEALTH as _____ is to POVERTY.

6. PREDICTIONS are to WARNINGS as HARBINGERS are to _____.

7. MALEVOLENCE is to EVIL as _____ is to GOOD.

8. MOTHER is to DAUGHTER as PARENT is to _____.

9. SUPERNATURAL is to UNEARTHLY as _____ is to GHOST.

10. URBAN is to CITY as _____ is to COUNTRY.

11. _____ is to _____ as _____ is to _____.

12. _____ is to _____ as _____ is to _____.

Name _____

Vocabulary

Directions: Complete the sentence by picking the word that best fits into the blank.

1. After an unsuccessful day of begging, the street urchin decided to _____ a loaf of bread.

   (A) infuse   (B) delineate   (C) purloin   (D) detain   (E) allude

2. In "The Tell-Tale Heart," a nervous murderer fails to recognize the _____ of his heart.

   (A) lassitude   (B) palpitation   (C) languor   (D) diligence   (E) pertinacity

3. Students are expected to be on time to class and will be penalized for _____.

   (A) convalescence (B) perversity (C) antipathy (D) eulogy (E) dilatoriness

4. She attributes her recovery after a long illness to the _____ climate in Arizona.

   (A) salubrious   (B) invincible   (C) obdurate   (D) livid   (E) desolating

5. He took one look at her face and guessed from her sad _____ that her goldfish must have died.

   (A) fetter   (B) countenance (C) cabriolet   (D) league   (E) asylum

6. After the loud bang, the _____ kittens huddled in a corner of the cage.

   (A) ignominious (B) timorous   (C) singular   (D) obscure   (E) stupendous

7. If you want to waterproof your boots, apply this spray and they will be _____ to rain.

   (A) pensive   (B) hapless   (C) disconsolate (D) dormant   (E) impervious

8. Walking during the day is certainly a healthful activity but nighttime _____ can have its hazards.

   (A) habitation   (B) emigration   (C) encomium   (D) perambulation (E) advocate

9. In the event of _____, stand within the shelter at the bus stop if you wish to remain dry.

   (A) recompense   (B) inclemency   (C) malignity   (D) pinnacle   (E) oblivion

10. The guide at the OK Corral Dude Ranch handed the nervous guest the reins and assured her that "Wildfire" was completely _____ despite his name.

    (A) ephemeral   (B) dank   (C) docile   (D) depraved   (E) desponding

Antonyms

permanent	few	lovable	strength
irreproachability	immense	welcomed	adoration
obtuseness	refuse	dishonored	poverty
empty	extol	elation	immaculate
convince	aggravated	thorough	determined

Directions: Look in the antonym box for the word that means the opposite of the given word.

_____ 1. transitory

_____ 2. odious

_____ 3. sagacity

_____ 4. irresolute

_____ 5. minute

_____ 6. cursory

_____ 7. remissness

_____ 8. appeased

_____ 9. spurned

_____ 10. concede

_____ 11. execration

_____ 12. impotence

_____ 13. myriads

_____ 14. squalid

_____ 15. dissuade

Synonyms

dreadful	continuous	dismay	dominant
enemy	imagine	curses	stopped
bloody	listlessness	drink	blaze
imitate	meal	insurmountable	schemes
unavoidable	prudent	wariness	whitecaps

Directions: For each of the words listed below, find a synonym in the synonym box.

_____ 1. inexorable

_____ 2. politic

_____ 3. sanguinary

_____ 4. machinations

_____ 5. consternation

_____ 6. torpor

_____ 7. emulate

_____ 8. conjecture

_____ 9. repast

_____ 10. adversary

_____ 11. appalling

_____ 12. imprecations

_____ 13. draught

_____ 14. paramount

_____ 15. conflagration

Name _____

Pros and Cons

Directions: With a partner, discuss Victor Frankenstein's decision to destroy the female creature rather than give it to his first creation. What were some of the reasons the creature gave in favor of giving him a female? What were some other reasons Victor may have considered? Why did Victor originally hesitate to agree? What reasons did he have for destroying the female rather than handing her over?

Take turns writing reasons why Victor should give the creature a female (in the YES column) and reasons why he should not (in the NO column). Discuss your chart with another pair of students and try to reach a consensus (agreement) on whether or not Victor made the best decision in the end. A spokesperson for this group of four should then report the group's conclusion to the whole class. Dissenting views of other groups should be heard at this time.

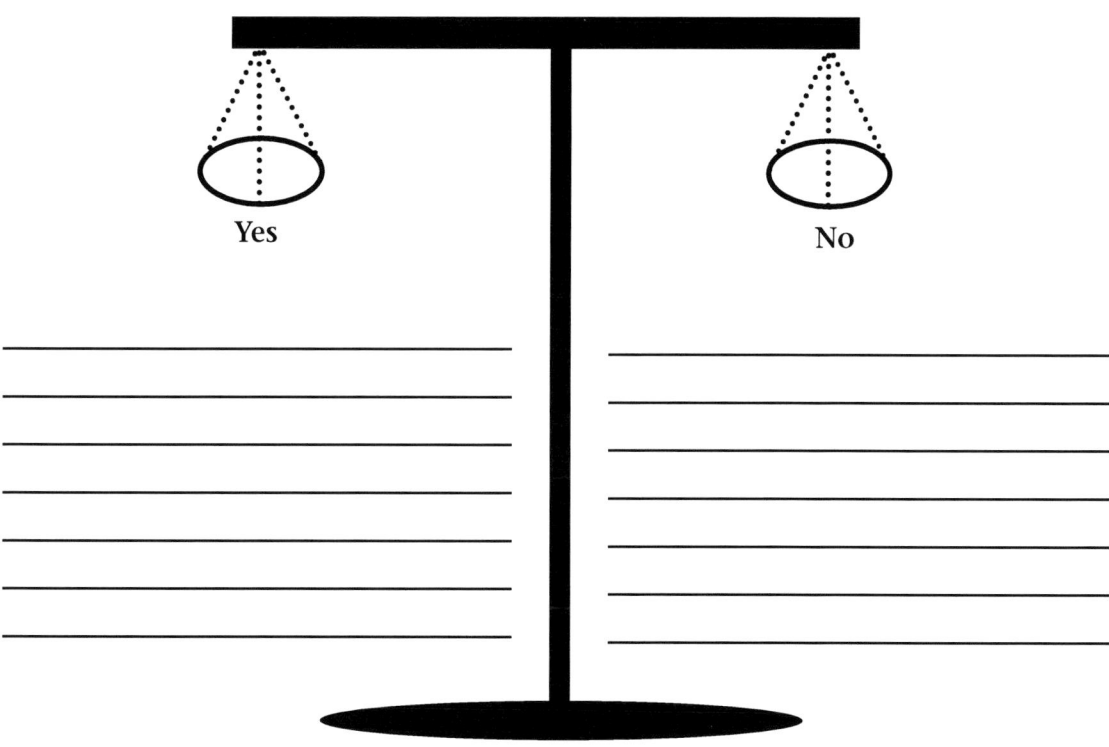

Yes   No

CONCLUSION: _____YES _____NO

On a separate sheet of paper, write an essay in which you explain and evaluate Victor's decision not to give the creature a female. Provide specific reasons why you do or do not agree that Victor did the right thing.

Critical Thinking

Directions: Two steps in problem-solving are 1) brainstorming possible solutions and 2) measuring each against specific criteria. When the creature kills William, Victor faces a problem. What should he do to prevent further killings? Help Victor solve his problem by:

  a) reading the choices in the chart below and adding others of your own creation
  b) measuring the choices against the criteria listed and one of your own that you add to the chart
  c) scoring each possible decision: 1=Yes! 2=Maybe... 3=No!

Possible Choices ↓	Criteria			
	Will this keep my friends and family alive?	Will this protect strangers?	Am I being a good "parent" to my creature?	
Tell my family why they are in danger.				
Stay close to those I care about.				
Hunt down and shoot the creature.				

I think the best choice is for Victor to _____

because _____.

Writing to Inform

Assignment: Write an essay comparing Captain Walton and Victor Frankenstein.

Pre-Writing: In a small group, complete the Venn diagram by listing words and phrases that describe each character below that character's name. Descriptive words that apply to both Walton and Frankenstein should go in the overlapping area.

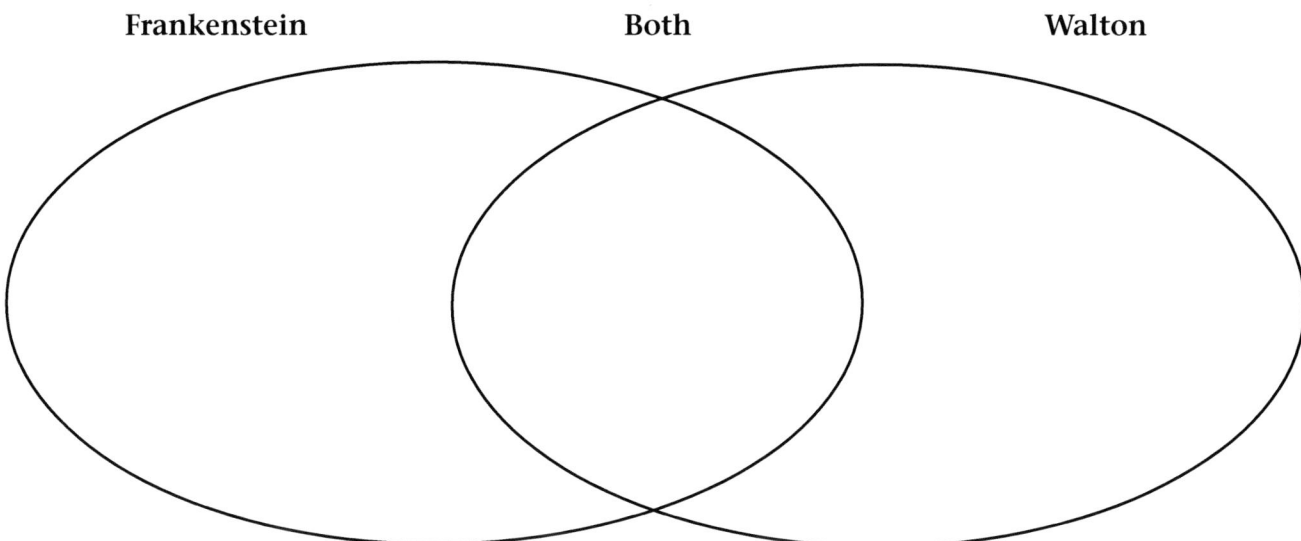

Frankenstein   Both   Walton

During Writing: On your own, write an essay in which you compare and contrast the characters of Walton and Frankenstein.

1. Answer some of these questions: How were their childhoods alike? What interests did they share as boys? Did they both have siblings? Were their fathers alike? What goals did each share? How did each want to be an innovator? Were both interested in doing something to benefit mankind? What words describe both men? Did they share some common weaknesses? Did they face similar dilemmas? Did they make different choices?

2. Decide how you will organize your ideas. Does it make sense to describe first one man and then the other? Or will you describe how they are similar, then how they are different?

3. Use some of the following transitional words and phrases to connect your ideas: also, alike, both, common, equally, in the same way, just as/so, likewise, same, too, similar, similarly, although, but differ, different, however, in contrast, on the other hand, unlike, whereas, while.

4. Incorporate details from the diagram as you develop and support your statements about each character.

Post-Writing: Share your essay with members of your group. Ask for comments, particularly on focus (whether you adhered to the topic), support (whether you provided enough reasons and examples in support of your statements) and organization (whether you grouped ideas together in a logical way).

I. FRAMEWORK STORY

A framework story is a "story within a story"—a convention used in such classical writing as the *Arabian Nights* and *The Canterbury Tales*.

A. Briefly explain the situation that "frames" the main story in the first 16 pages. Who is speaking?

B. Who tells most of the main story, which begins with Chapter 1?

C. At what point does the main story serve as a frame for someone else's story?

D. Does the main story return to the frame situation at the end?

II. DOPPELGÄNGER

This term ("ghostly double") refers to a ghostly counterpart of a living person. Hawthorne and Poe are among the many writers who have used this device, commonly to dramatize the dual nature—the "good" and "bad" selves—of a particular character.

Some critics maintain that the creature represents the scientist's "bad" self. What hidden, subconscious reasons might Frankenstein have for desiring each of the deaths caused by the creature?

A. William

B. Justine

C. Clerval

D. Elizabeth

E. Victor's father

III. ALLUSION

An allusion is a reference to a person, place, event, or artistic work—often from literature, history, scripture, or mythology—which the author expects the reader to recognize.

Directions: Identify the speaker and briefly explain each allusion below. Describe the connection between the original reference and Shelley's story.

A. p. 7: "I shall kill no albatross; therefore do not be alarmed for my safety or if I should come back to you as worn and woeful as the 'Ancient Mariner.' "

B. p. 84: "I ought to be thy Adam, but I am rather the fallen angel, whom thou drivest from joy for no misdeed."

C. p. 90: "...it presented to me then as exquisite and divine a retreat as Pandemonium appeared to the demons of hell after their sufferings in the lake of fire"

Newspaper

Prewriting:

1. Reread the sections of the novel that describe Justine's trial and execution.

2. Using the text and your imagination, summarize what happened. (Who was involved? What did these persons do? When did it happen? Where did it happen? How did it happen? Why did it happen?)

During Writing: Write the newspaper article that appeared the day after the execution. (Try to include some eyewitness accounts and some direct quotes.)

After Writing:

1. Give your article a headline.

2. Give your newspaper a name.

3. Draw or cut out a "photo" to accompany your story.

4. Read the article aloud to a partner or group.

Name _____

Letter

Directions: Suppose that you are the creature. You decide to write to "Gabby"—a syndicated advice columnist—using a disguised name and address.

Part I: Finish the letter below.

Dear Gabby:

I never imagined I'd be writing to a complete stranger about my problems, but I have no one else to turn to. I feel such a sense of despair, but I don't think there is anything you can say to help me. First of all, I hate the way I look...

I have no friends...

Even my father can't stand me...

The idea of getting someone to go out with me is a joke...

Please tell me what to do, or I'm afraid I'll...

Signed,

_____ in _____
        (assumed name)   (location)

Part II: In a small group, brainstorm various pieces of advice that Gabby might give the writer. Then write the letter that appears as an answer in her column. (Use the back of your paper for Gabby's answer.)

Critical Thinking

Directions: Watch the Kenneth Branagh version of *Mary Shelley's Frankenstein* (1994). Write a review of the movie. Include a comparison of the movie and the book. What changes were made to the story? What scenes or characters were added, deleted, condensed, changed? Why do you suppose the changes were made? Did the changes enhance the quality of the story or detract from it?

Use this framework to take notes on the book and the movie. The framework is designed to help you organize your ideas before writing the review.

The title of the film is _____. It was made in _____,

stars _____

_____, and was directed by _____.

What I Liked About the Film		What I Disliked About the Film	

Opening Scene		Key Characters	
Book	Movie	Book	Movie

Memorable Lines	
Book	Movie

Nature of Relationships between Characters	
Book	Movie
Creature/Creator	
Frankenstein/Female	
Frankenstein/Clerval	
Frankenstein/Elizabeth	

Final Scene	
Book	Movie

Crucial Events	
Book	Movie

Key Settings	
Book	Movie

Current Events

Directions: In a small group, match each of the characters and situations below with one or more people/situations that have come up in recent news (political, entertainment, etc.).

Flip through recent issues of newspapers and news magazines for ideas. (If you're feeling creative, choose one of your matches and use it as the basis for a political cartoon.)

Sample: Senator Packwood's diaries and Victor Frankenstein's journals—both were private documents that proved incriminating when they got into the "wrong hands."

Novel	News
Victor Frankenstein	
the creature	
Elizabeth	
Justine	
William	
the Cottagers	
the murders	
the adoptions	
learning to read and write	
parenting	
letters from the captain, Elizabeth	

Literary Analysis

Directions: The chart on this page will help you understand the conflicts Victor and the creature undergo and their motivation for acting as they do. In the rectangles for each character, explain how the action might be seen as evil or wrong—and how it might not.

Incident	Evil/Wrong	Not Evil/Wrong
1. In college, Victor became so obsessed with his work on animation that he failed to write to his family.		
2. When the creature first opened his eyes, Victor ran away.		
3. When the creature disappeared, Victor did not tell anyone about his creation, then fell into a two-month nervous fever.		
4. After Clerval nursed Victor back to health, Victor did not tell him about the creature.		
5. When Victor realized that the creature had murdered William, he did not tell anyone that he had created a monster.		
6. When Justine stood accused, Victor did not reveal what he knew about the creature.		
7. The creature killed William after William screamed.		
8. Victor began to create a female, then destroyed it.		
9. Victor married Elizabeth and failed to warn or protect her despite the creature's threat.		
10. Victor encouraged the sailors to continue on, risking their lives—and urged the Captain not to meet their demands to return to safety.		

Use your notes to write an essay on "Goodness and Evil in Mary Shelley's *Frankenstein*." Was Victor evil? Why was he so intent on creating a human being? Why wasn't he a better "father" to his creation? Why didn't he protect his family and friends? Was the creature evil?

Name _____

Crossword

Directions: Use the clues on pp. 24–25 to complete the puzzle.

Across

2. Victor was fascinated by _____ like Paracelsus.

4. The creature demanded that Victor make one.

7. Victor's soulmate and bride

9. The captain who was driven by some of the same desires as Victor Frankenstein.

10. The author of Frankenstein is Mary _____.

12. The creature called the cottagers his _____.

15. Victor often refers to the creature as the _____.

16. Where Victor placed the torn remains of the female creature

Across, cont.

18. He made the creature.

19. Country where the creature took up residence in a hovel near the DeLacey's cottage.

21. Where Victor's family lived

22. Where Victor tried to find peace after Justine's death

23. The incriminating evidence found in Justine's pocket

27. Where Victor's parents were staying when he was born

28. Walton complained to his sister that he didn't have one.

29. She was executed even though she was innocent of murder.

30. What the creature and Victor both drove across the ice

31. Where Victor went to pursue his studies

Down

1. The creature was enraged when William hurled these at him.

2. One of the cottagers, Felix's sister

3. Elizabeth begged the crowd not to let Justine perish there.

5. "You are my creator, but I am your _____."

6. The ship was surrounded by this.

7. Victor's surviving brother

8. The cottagers were imprisoned and impoverished for helping a _____.

11. Victor's murdered brother

13. Victor spent a lot of time in _____ houses getting body parts.

14. The creature learned to read by watching the cottagers instruct her.

15. The cottager who thought he was defending his father

17. The novel opens with four of these destined for Mrs. Saville.

18. "And now it is ended; there is my last _____."

20. This drove the creature after Felix beat him and the cottagers left.

24. Victor became interested in galvanism after seeing lightning strike this.

25. The creature approached the senior DeLacey because he was _____.

26. Walton became one for a year.

Name _____

A. True/False: Mark each with a *T* for true or an *F* for false.

_____ 1. Walton is trying to find a more direct route to the North Pole.

_____ 2. The story takes place during the early 1900's.

_____ 3. Walton meets Victor Frankenstein while interviewing sailors to be on his crew.

_____ 4. Elizabeth was raised by a peasant family before being adopted by Victor's parents.

_____ 5. Victor's mother died after nursing Elizabeth through a bout of scarlet fever.

_____ 6. Victor became fascinated by galvanism after seeing lightning kill a horse.

_____ 7. Victor's best friend, Clerval, went off with Victor to study anatomy at Ingolstadt.

_____ 8. After opening his eyes for the first time, the creature became enraged and tried to strangle Victor.

_____ 9. After bringing the creature to life, Victor spent the next two months trying to hunt him down.

_____ 10. After William's murder, Victor cast suspicion on Justine to draw attention away from himself.

_____ 11. People thought that Justine had stolen a locket with a picture of Victor's mother.

_____ 12. Justine confessed to William's murder and was executed.

_____ 13. When the creature joined Victor on the glacier, Victor restrained himself from trying to kill his creation.

_____ 14. Victor overcame the creature's objections and convinced him to tell his creator what his life had been like.

_____ 15. The creature told Victor that when he entered a cottage looking for food, the villagers chased him.

B. Matching: Match each cause in the left column to the correct effect in the right column.

____ 1. The blind father played a guitar.

____ 2. Victor was in despair after Justine's death.

____ 3. Victor searched his apartment for the creature he had just brought to life.

____ 4. Victor wanted to animate dead matter.

____ 5. Victor saw an oak blasted to bits.

a. He rode to the valley of Chamounix, where he had found peace as a boy.

b. He was overjoyed to find the monster gone.

c. The creature was moved by the music.

d. He was frantic when he couldn't locate the creature.

e. He spends a lot of time in charnel-houses.

f. The creature became enraged and broke the instrument.

g. He attempted suicide.

h. He developed an early fascination with electricity.

A. Fill-Ins: Fill in each blank with the word or phrase that makes the statement true.

The novel opens with a letter written by explorer 1. _____ to his

2. _____ in England, sometime during the 3. _____'s. He reports that he has arrived

in Russia and is confident that he will succeed in his plan to 4. _____

_____. A few months later, he writes about a

strange occurrence. While the ship was 5. _____ the men saw a

gigantic 6. _____. A few hours later, the sailors rescued a stranger by

7. _____. The stranger explained that he had been

8. _____. Over the next few weeks, Walton and

the stranger became 9. _____ and the stranger told him about his past. The

stranger's childhood had been a(n) 10. _____ one. When he was five, his parents adopted

11. _____ and Victor quickly grew to feel that she

12. _____. In school, Victor's best friend was an

adventurous boy named 13. _____ _____. After seeing an oak blasted

by lightning, Victor 14. _____.

B. Short Answer: Respond to each item below.

15. How did Victor's mother die?

_____

_____

16. Why was the day that Victor met M. Waldman at Ingolstadt "a day memorable to me; it decided my future destiny"?

_____

_____

17. Why did Victor decide to make his human being gigantic?

_____

_____

18. How did Victor change while he was working on the creature?

_____

_____

19. Why wasn't Victor pleased with his creation when he finished?

_____

_____

20. How did Clerval prove himself to be a good friend during the months after Victor created the monster?

_____

_____

21. In what way was Victor responsible for Justine's death?

_____

_____

22. Why didn't Victor kill the creature after William's murder?

_____

_____

23. What do you think is the most convincing point the creature makes in arguing for Victor to make a female?

_____

_____

24. Name one detail that sticks out in your mind from the creature's description of his first few weeks of existence.

_____

_____

© Novel Units, Inc.

A. Identification: Match each quote in the left column to the correct speaker in the right column.

____ 1. Victor's little brother, "with sweet laughing blue eyes"

____ 2. Victor's "more than sister"

____ 3. She was executed for William's murder.

____ 4. A kindly blind cottager whose guitar-playing pleased the creature

____ 5. Victor's friend, "a boy of singular talent and fancy"

____ 6. "I became capable of bestowing animation upon lifeless matter."

____ 7. The beautiful Turkish woman who followed Felix to his cottage in Germany

____ 8. The teacher who welcomed Victor as a "disciple" and urged him to study all branches of science

____ 9. The explorer who befriended Victor and listened to his tale

____ 10. He doesn't realize the creature does not intend to hurt his father.

a. R. Walton

b. Victor Frankenstein

c. Elizabeth

d. William

e. Clerval

f. M. Waldman

g. Justine

h. De Lacey, Sr.

i. Safie

j. Felix

B. Multiple Choice: Choose the BEST answer.

____ 11. Which is NOT a reason Walton writes to his sister?
    a. to reassure her that he is safe
    b. to share the stranger's tale
    c. to request that she send money

____ 12. When they were boys, Victor and Walton both were
    a. eager to learn
    b. lonely and without friends
    c. motherless children

____ 13. Victor tells his story to Walton so that Walton will
    a. publish it
    b. take him back to London
    c. avoid some of Victor's mistakes

____ 14. Victor describes both his mother and Elizabeth as
    a. brilliant
    b. merciful
    c. tough

____ 15. Before rescuing Victor, the sailors look through their telescopes and are amazed to see
   a. the North Pole
   b. a house in flames
   c. the creature

____ 16. While Victor explored the way things work, his friend Clerval preferred to
   a. write and act out tales of chivalry
   b. figure out ways to earn money
   c. play competitive sports

____ 17. When the creature first opened his eyes, Victor experienced
   a. disgust
   b. delight
   c. sorrow

____ 18. After his new creature disappeared and again after Clerval was killed, Victor
   a. fell into a nervous fever
   b. put all of his energy into capturing the creature
   c. attempted suicide

____ 19. Frankenstein told his father that he felt responsible for the deaths of
   a. his mother, William, and Clerval
   b. William, Justine, and Clerval
   c. his teacher, William, and Clerval

____ 20. The creature promised to stop hurting people if Victor would
   a. promise not to marry Elizabeth
   b. spend more time with him
   c. make a female for him

____ 21. The deal the creature made with Victor is most like the deal
   a. the United States made with Great Britain in the Treaty of Paris (ending the Revolutionary War)
   b. Franklin Delano Roosevelt made with the American people (during the Depression)
   c. the Unabomber made with the editors of *The Washington Post* and *The New York Times* (September, 1995)

____ 22. Victor promised to tell Elizabeth everything
   a. on Valentine's Day
   b. the day after their wedding
   c. the day of his graduation

____ 23. Victor left his bride alone despite the creature's warning because Victor
   a. thought the creature intended to kill him
   b. was using Elizabeth as a lure
   c. could not bear to see his beloved murdered

____ 24. Frankenstein's father died
      a. of strangulation at the hands of the creature
      b. of grief soon after Elizabeth's murder
      c. on the scaffold after William's death

____ 25. After Elizabeth's death, Victor traveled to the North Country in search of
      a. revenge
      b. knowledge
      c. peace

____ 26. Near death, Victor exhorts the crew to
      a. change course and pursue the creature
      b. change course and go home to safety
      c. continue on their course and not give up

____ 27. When the sailors ask Walton to promise that he will head home when they are free of the ice, he
      a. agrees to head home
      b. threatens to have them jailed for mutiny
      c. laughs in their faces

____ 28. When the creature finds his master dead, he expresses
      a. suspicion that Walton had murdered Victor
      b. grief that his beloved creator was gone
      c. anger that he could no longer make Victor suffer

____ 29. If Victor had still been alive when the creature arrived, which of the following would MOST LIKELY have happened?
      a. The creature would have killed Victor.
      b. Captain Walton would have killed the creature.
      c. The creature would have spoken to Victor and left.

____ 30. At the end, the creature cries out that he is going off to
      a. die
      b. seek revenge
      c. live by himself in peace

Name _____

A. Identification: On a separate sheet of paper, explain who each character is and briefly describe him or her in one or two sentences.

1. Walton

2. Victor Frankenstein

3. Elizabeth

4. William

5. Clerval

6. M. Waldman

7. Justine

8. De Lacey, Sr.

9. Safie

10. Felix

B. Short Answer: On a separate sheet of paper, answer each question in complete sentences.

11. Why does Victor Frankenstein tell Captain Walton this story?

12. Why didn't Victor's family hear from him for several months after he went off to study at Ingolstadt?

13. What happened on that night when Victor succeeded in bringing the creature to life?

14. Why was Justine executed for William's murder?

15. Why did the creature kill William?

16. List three reasons the creature liked the De Lacey family.

17. How did the creature plan to be accepted by the De Lacey family—and why didn't the plan work?

18. Describe three acts of kindness by the creature.

19. Why was Victor suspected in Clerval's death? Why do you suppose Clerval was not executed on the basis of "circumstantial evidence"—and Justine was?

20. Why did Victor make a female—then destroy her?

21. Why did Victor marry Elizabeth despite the creature's threat about his wedding night?

C. Quotations: Briefly identify each quote. (Paraphrase the quote and tell who was speaking—and to whom.)

22. "I was easily led by the sympathy which he evinced to use the language of my heart to give utterance to the burning ardour of my soul, and to say, with all the fervour that warmed me, how gladly I would sacrifice my fortune, my existence, my every hope, to the furtherance of my enterprise."

_____

_____

23. "It was on a dreary night of November that I beheld the accomplishment of my toils."

_____

_____

24. "Dear lady, I had none to support me; all looked on me as a wretch doomed to ignominy and perdition. What could I do? In an evil hour I subscribed to a lie; and now only am I truly miserable."

_____

_____

25. "This was then the reward of my benevolence! I had saved a human being from destruction, and as a recompense I now writhed under the miserable pain of a wound which shattered the flesh and bone."

_____

_____

26. "I swear to you, by the earth which I inhabit, and by you that made me, that with the companion you bestow I will quit the neighborhood of man and dwell, as it may chance, in the most savage of places."

_____

_____

27. "Slave, I before reasoned with you, but you have proved yourself unworthy of my condescension...You are my creator, but I am your master; obey!"

_____

_____

28. "I have devoted my creator, the select specimen of all that is worthy of love and admiration among men, to misery; I have pursued him even to that irremediable ruin. There he lies, white and cold in death. You hate me, but your abhorrence cannot equal that with which I regard myself."

_____

_____

D. Essay

29. **Analysis:** Select A, B, or C and respond in a well-organized essay on a separate sheet of paper.

   A. Describe Victor Frankenstein's strengths and weaknesses.

   B. Explain what Captain Walton has learned from Victor Frankenstein's example.

   C. Analyze how Shelley builds suspense throughout the story. (Consider the questions she raises in the reader's mind and the way she describes various settings.)

30. **Critical/Creative Thinking:** Select A, B, or C and respond in a well-organized essay on a separate sheet of paper.

   A. In the end, do you feel more sympathy for the creature or for Victor? Why?

   B. Victor asks himself (p. 131): "...did I not as his maker owe him all the portion of happiness that it was in my power to bestow?" Write Victor a letter telling him why you do or do not agree with his conclusion. Use supportive evidence from your own experience and/or reading to defend your opinion. Advise Victor on what you think he should do about the unhappy creature he has created.

   C. Assume the persona of Victor. Write a monologue revealing your thoughts as you come upon your dead master (before the entrance of Captain Walton).

Answer Key

Activities #1 and #2: Students should be given time to discuss their answers with a partner or in a group.

Study Guide
Letters 1–4

1. Walton is an explorer seeking a new route to the North Pole. He is writing to his sister to reassure her that he is all right and to describe the stranger he has met.

2. He loved to read his uncle's books about voyages of discovery.

3. He tried being a poet.

4. He has not found a friend.

5. He was struck by the man's kindness, integrity, courage. (When the woman whose hand he had been promised told him she was in love with someone else, he let her go and gave his rival money to establish a farm.)

6. They saw a gigantic figure going over the ice in a dog-drawn sledge.

7. He was in poor condition and would presumably want to be rescued no matter what.

8. He said that he was looking for someone who had fled from him.

9. Walton is attracted to the man's amiability, gentleness, and eloquent way with words.

Chapters 1–4

1. His father was protective of the younger woman he had married—Victor's mother.

2. They doted on him, were deeply conscious of their duties as parents to help him be happy.

3. Elizabeth's German mother had died giving birth to her and her father had given her to the peasants to raise before he died or was imprisoned. The peasant family then fell on hard times and decided it would be better for her to live with Victor's mother, who happened to visit them.

4. They returned to Switzerland.

5. Victor's one close friend was Henry Clerval.

6. He saw an old oak blasted by lightning.

7. After nursing Elizabeth through scarlet fever, Victor's mother herself caught it and died.

8. M. Waldman, a teacher who specialized in chemistry, welcomed his new student.

9. He knew how to bring matter to life but now had to figure out how to construct a human body. He may have spoken in a slightly awed tone.

Chapters 5–7

1. He ran from the laboratory and paced in his bedroom, slept for a few nightmarish moments, jumped up when the creature held up the curtain of the bed, paced in the courtyard.

2. He didn't tell Clerval about the experiments, but raved while in a nervous fever.

3. If Clerval hadn't nursed him back to health during the months of "nervous fever," Victor would have died.

4. Justine has returned to Victor's family, following the death of her mother. Elizabeth reminds Victor that Justine's widowed, verbally abusive mother allowed the girl to live in Victor's household from age 12 on, then called her home after the deaths of her siblings.

5. They studied the writings of the Orientalists.

6. He had just spent a couple of happy weeks on a walking tour with his friend, Clerval.

7. William was murdered while hiding from his brother, Ernest.

8. Victor returned to Geneva and caught a glimpse of the creature during a flash of lightning.

9. Maybe they would think he was having a nervous breakdown and imagining things.

Chapters 8–11

1. A locket with a picture of William's mother was found in her pocket—the same locket Elizabeth had put around his neck.

2. Elizabeth has lived in the same house with Justine for years, knows how attached she was to William and how kind she was to William's mother during her fatal illness.

3. Justine was pressured to confess and wanted absolution; she was hanged.

4. Victor wanted to avenge the deaths of Justine and William—but seemed to doubt that he could kill the creature.

5. Victor took a trip to the Alps to calm himself and met the creature; he sprang at the creature, who eluded him.

6. If Victor would create a female for him, the creature would go off with her and leave mankind alone.

7. He had wandered through the woods, frightened, hungry, and cold. Villagers had chased and beaten him and he had taken refuge in a hovel near a cottage.

8. In the cottage lived a blind old man and his adult children—a loving but poor family.

9. Sample: "The silver hair and benevolent countenance of the aged cottager won my reverence..." p. 93; "the younger was slight and graceful in his figure, and his features were moulded with the finest symmetry..." p. 93

Chapters 12–15

1. When the creature saw the younger cottagers giving their food to their grandfather, he realized that they sometimes went hungry; he was moved by their kindness.

2. He listened carefully to the cottagers' speech.

3. He observed as the cottagers taught Safie.

4. He saw his reflection in a pool.

5. He gathered firewood for them and cleared snow.

6. Safie, the Turkish woman he loved, appeared.

7. They were imprisoned and had their property taken when their role in helping Safie's father get out of prison was discovered.

8. He was moved by it, saw parallels to his own situation, resented that his "father" didn't support him as God protected Adam.

9. Personal Response

Chapters 16–19

1. The creature returned to try to win over the old man; he found the cottage still and later overheard Felix tell his landlord the family could never again live in the cottage.

2. He decided to find Victor in Geneva.

3. He rescued a girl who had fallen into the water and was shot by the man who grabbed the girl from him.

4. He met William and strangled him after the boy screamed, cursed him, revealed that he was Victor's brother.

5. He was enraged by the thought that women like Victor's mother or Justine would never smile on him so he decided to make her "atone" by framing her.

6. The two might unite in wickedness to wreak even greater havoc on the world.

7. Victor decided that the creature was right—as his creator, Victor owed it to him to give him a companion—so Victor decided to create a female.

8. He didn't want to corrupt his home by doing such vile work there so he decided to go to England where he would have better access to the knowledge he needed.

9. Sample: "...it became every day more horrible and irksome to me."—p. 149

Chapters 20–22

1. Together the pair might have children; she might detest and desert him, leaving him more angry than ever.

2. Victor saw the look of malice, realized he was wrong to create the female, and tore the project to pieces.

3. Victor assumed that the creature would murder him when he got married.

4. The stranger thought that Victor was a murderer.

5. He was strangled by the creature.

6. He again fell into a nervous fever.

7. Mr. Kirwin, the magistrate, was a kind old man who provided him with a physician and nurse and ultimately helped set Victor free.

8. Victor's father was overjoyed, but Elizabeth had a presentiment of something evil.

9. Sample: Clerval probably would have lived.

Chapters 23–24

1. Victor realized what the creature's warning had really meant: The creature had come to kill not him but Elizabeth on their wedding night.

2. He was despondent and died a few days later.

3. He sought help in capturing the creature.

4. He was hunting the creature to exact revenge.

5. Victor assumed that the creature didn't want him to give up his search or die because that would deprive the creature of the chance to torment him.

6. Victor wants Walton to promise to kill the creature, not to trust him or he may hurt others.

7. Victor tells the men not to be cowards but Walton agrees to turn back.

8. The creature was grief-stricken, filled with remorse.

9. The creature's words made the captain feel some compassion for the creature. The creature promised to leave the ship, head north, and die there; then he jumped out of the ship onto an ice raft and was swept away. Walton was a humane person who probably believed the creature's avowal that he was no longer a threat; besides, the captain didn't have much time to think before the creature was gone.

Activity #3: 1. transmuted 2. sepulchre 3. panegyric 4. galvanism 5. penury 6. forebodings 7. benevolence 8. progeny 9. apparition 10. rustic 11.–12. Answers will vary.

Activity #4: 1. C 2. B 3. E 4. A 5. B. 6. B 7. E 8. D 9. B 10. C

Activity #5: 1. permanent 2. lovable 3. obtuseness 4. determined 5. immense 6. thorough 7. irreproachability 8. aggravated 9. welcomed 10. refuse 11. adoration 12. strength 13. few 14. immaculate 15. convince

Activity #6: 1. unavoidable 2. prudent 3. bloody 4. schemes 5. dismay 6. listlessness 7. imitate 8. imagine 9. meal 10. enemy 11. dreadful 12. curses 13. drink 14. dominant 15. blaze

Activity #7: Answers will vary; should include—YES: He owes the creature a measure of happiness; the creature may leave humans alone; NO: Together they might have children; they might not get along anyway, which would further enrage the creature.

Activity #8: Answers will vary.

Activity #9: Answers will vary. Essays should refer to the fact that both men face ethical dilemmas in their quest for knowledge/innovation.

Activity #10: I. A. Captain Walton is writing to his sister about his voyage—and sharing with her the story the stranger tells him. B. Victor Frankenstein C. The creature's tale as told to Victor begins with Chapter 11 D. Yes, we return to the captain's narration. **II.** Sample answers: A. sibling rivalry B. jealousy of the attention his parents gave to this girl, whom they took into the family C. jealousy; Clerval—enthusiastic, good—was many things that Victor was not. D. Elizabeth—sibling rivalry; She had a special place in Victor's father's heart; his mother died after tending her. E. Victor's father—Oedipal jealousy **III.** A. *The Rime of the Ancient Mariner* (Coleridge)—Walton is reassuring his sister by telling her that he isn't like the miserable sailor in the poem, for whom the albatross was a recurrent sign of bad luck. B. The creature berates his master by comparing his situation to the biblical one described in *Paradise Lost*—except that his creator has punished him wrongfully by deserting him. C. The creature is describing how wonderful the shepherd's hut appeared after living in the woods for weeks; he compares it to the capital of Hell in *Paradise Lost*, where the demons sought refuge.

Activities #11 and #12: Answers will vary.

Activity #13: Answers will vary. (Encourage students to discuss differences between the novel and the movie first. For example, in the movie the monster is created from the body of a cholera victim who kills Victor's beloved teacher and the female is created from Elizabeth's body after the creature takes out her heart; Victor's mother dies in childbirth with William—not as a result of nursing Elizabeth during her illness; the creature murders Frankenstein's father—he doesn't just die of grief.)

Activities #14 and #15: Answers will vary.

Activity #16:

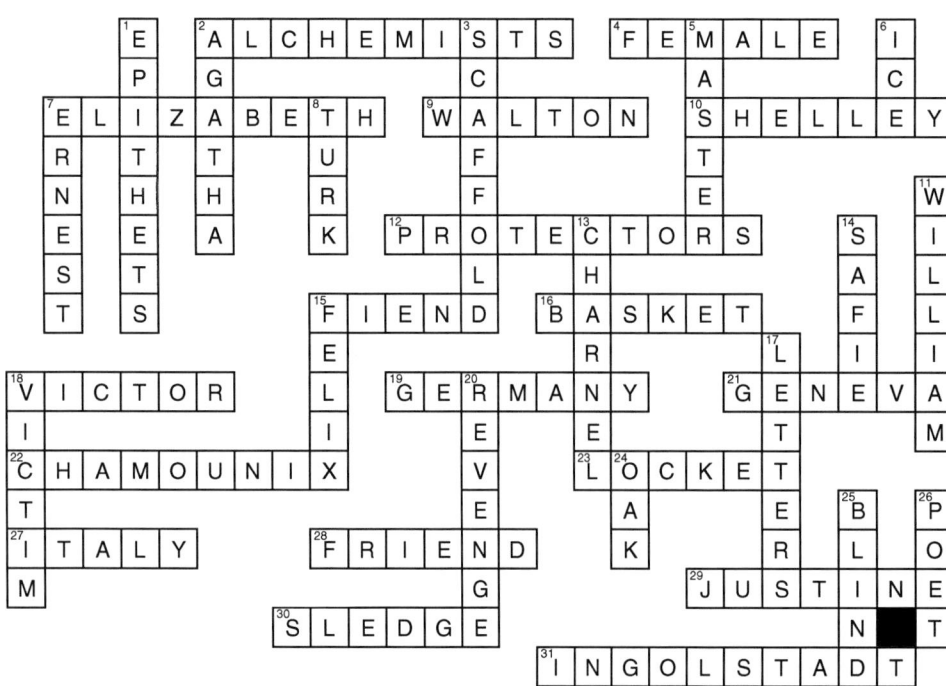

| © Novel Units, Inc.

Comprehension Quiz, Level I

A. 1. T 2. F 3. F 4. T 5. T 6. F 7. F 8. F 9. F 10. F 11. T 12. T 13. F 14. F 15. T

B. 16. c 17. a 18. b 19. e 20. h

Comprehension Quiz, Level II

A. 1. Walton 2. sister 3. 1700 4. find a new route to the North Pole 5. trapped by ice 6. creature in a dog-drawn sledge racing over the ice 7. pulling him off a chunk of ice onto the ship 8. chasing someone who had fled from him 9. friends 10 happy 11. a girl named Elizabeth 12. was more than a sister 13. Henry Clerval 14. became fascinated by the study of electricity. **B.** 15. She nursed Elizabeth through a bout with scarlet fever, then caught it herself. 16. Victor became the teacher's disciple and learned much about science from him; he applied what he learned and was able to bring lifeless matter to life. 17. Working with small parts hindered Victor's ability to work quickly. 18. He became obsessed, lost touch with his family, lost weight, grew pale. 19. He had planned something beautiful and was disgusted by the ugly result. 20. He nursed Victor back to health when Victor fell into a nervous fever. 21. The creature created by Victor "framed" Justine and she was subsequently executed. 22. He did spring at the creature, but the creature eluded him. 23. Sample: Victor owes his creation a measure of happiness. 24. Sample: He was delighted by the singing of the birds.

Novel Test, Level I

A. 1. D 2. C 3. G 4. H 5. E 6. B 7. I 8. F 9. A 10. J **B.** 11. C 12. A 13. C 14. B 15. C 16. A 17. A 18. A 19. B 20. C 21. C 22. B 23. A 24. B 25. A 26. C 27. A 28. B 29. C 30. A

Novel Test, Level II

A. 1. Walton is the captain who is seeking a new route to the North Pole. He shares Victor's tale with his sister in a letter. 2. Victor Frankenstein is the scientist who makes and deserts the creature, then suffers as the creature kills his loved ones. 3. Elizabeth is the kind, gentle adopted sister Frankenstein loves—and marries. 4. William is Victor's curly-haired little brother, the creature's first victim. 5. Clerval is Victor's kind, exuberant, romantic best friend—and one of the creature's victims. 6. M. Waldman is the science teacher who acts as Frankenstein's mentor. 7. Justine is the kind, innocent girl who is accused of William's murder and dies on the scaffold. 8. De Lacey is the kind, blind cottager whose guitar-playing the creature enjoys; he speaks kindly when the creature approaches him alone. 9. Safie is the lovely turk with whom Felix is in love. 10. Felix is the young man at the cottage who took pity on Safie's father. **B.** 11. Frankenstein recognizes a kindred spirit in Captain Walton, who is driven by the idea of acquiring new knowledge at any cost, and hopes to help him avoid some of his own mistakes. 12. He isolated himself while working on his animation experiments. 13. He ran to his bedroom in disgust and paced there, then fell into a feverish sleep. When the creature came to his bedside, Victor ran out into the courtyard. 14. She was found to have the locket that Elizabeth had placed around William's neck shortly before he disappeared. 15. The creature wanted to befriend the boy, but the boy made him angry by screaming—and revealed that he was a relative of the creature's enemy, Victor. 16. Sample: He saw that the young people took care of the old man; he enjoyed their physical beauty; he was touched by the way Felix brought his sister a flower. 17. He planned to befriend the old man first, and through him—the others. Felix interrupted the first meeting and beat the creature. 18. Sample: The creature gathered wood for the cottagers, cleared the snow for them, rescued a young girl from drowning. 19. Witnesses had seen a boat like his near the scene of the crime. Perhaps the crowd in Geneva was more bloodthirsty because the victim was a child they knew. 20. At first he thought that the female might appease the creature but he had second thoughts when he saw the creature's malicious expression. 21. He didn't realize that her life was in danger; he thought the creature was threatening him—not his bride-to-be—and that the sooner the wedding date, the sooner the creature would stop attacking others. **C.** 22. Captain Walton is telling his sister that he felt comfortable telling the stranger how much he was willing to risk to succeed in finding the route to the North Pole. 23. Victor is telling the captain about the night he brought the creature to life. 24. Justine is explaining to Elizabeth that she confessed to the murder of William because everyone acted as if she would be doomed in the hereafter, otherwise. 25. The creature is complaining to Victor about how he was shot after rescuing the girl from drowning. 26. The creature is promising Victor that he will leave mankind alone only if Victor will give him a female to go off with. 27. The creature is warning Victor that he had better do as he says and make a female. 28. The creature is talking to the captain, bemoaning the fact that he made his dead master's life miserable, saying that he hates himself more than the captain ever could. **D. 29. A.** Students who select A might mention that Frankenstein enjoys learning, works hard, wants to add to the world's store of knowledge but that he acts without considering the consequences, neglects those who love him, deserts his creation, feels sorry for himself. **B.** Students who select B should discuss the fact that Walton's decision not to endanger his men might be due in part to seeing how Frankenstein's single-mindedness resulted in the deaths of innocents. **C.** Students who answer C might mention the gloomy settings (the laboratory, the charnel houses, the misty cemetery, etc.), Elizabeth's premonitions, comments made by Victor that foreshadow something terrible ahead in his story (e.g., "Destiny was too potent, and her immutable laws had decreed my utter and terrible destruction"—p. 27). 30. **A.–C.** Personal Response. Answers should include details from the story as well as from students' imaginations.

Notes

Notes